the last laugh

fighting cancer with wit and humor

ROBBY LEE FELDMAN

© 2005 Robby Lee Feldman. All rights reserved.

This book may not be reproduced in any form without express written permission.
Printed in the United States of America
ISBN 1-58385-065-1

*Dedicated to everyone who has
the will, strength and resilience to fight illness with humor.
For those who don't, may this book inspire you to do so.*

The neurosurgeon, with a pensive and foreboding expression on his face, solemnly told my 83-year-old Mom, Eleanor, that she had a brain tumor the size of a golf ball. Mom barely blinked and said, "I never did like golf."

prologue

Eleanor P. Feldman was born July 3rd, 1920, a few hours before the fireworks started for Independence Day. No wonder she's been so fiercely independent. And so fond of fireworks.

Legend has it that the first sign of her independence and strong will was when the birthing doctor slapped her and she slapped back.

Yeah, my Mom has a long list of good traits. Insight. Intelligence. Loyalty. Bravery. Persistence. Patience. Practicality. Oh, and she never, ever complains. But nothing stands out as much as her sense of humor. Mom has always been funny. Very funny.

Sometimes, she uses her humor as a way to put people at ease. Sometimes to deflect attention from an awkward situation. Sometimes simply because it puts a little extra joy in life.

Lately, however, Mom has been using her honed sense of humor for another reason—to make dying a little bit easier. For her, sure. But mostly for the people around her. Because Mom believes that when people are smiling, maybe it alleviates some of the pain. Truth is, there's plenty of pain to go around for the folks who are fortunate enough to be part of Mom's life. And it's ironic, actually. She has brought so much humor into people's lives that it has made watching her debilitating illness that much more painful. If Mom were asked to comment on that irony, she'd probably say something like, "So you're telling me that humor can cause pain...that seems very inefficient," issuing it with her characteristic teenage-girl-like giggle.

There's a lot more you might want to know about my Mom. That she grew up in Philadelphia and moved eight times just during high school. That she married an Army soldier during World War II. That she raised four children. That she lost her husband when she was 47. That she survived breast cancer...twice.

No wonder she developed a sense of humor. If nothing else, it was strictly survival instinct. And the day she learned that she had brain cancer—most likely incurable—was the day she needed that humor more than any time in the past.

So did we.

note

Eleanor Feldman's four children, in birth order are Barry, Geri, Denis (D. Jay), and Robby. Eleanor lives in Tampa, as does D. Jay. Barry lives in Colorado, Geri in Virginia, Robby in Tennessee. In this book, they will often be referred to as Bar, Ger, D. Jay, and Rob. Mom would've liked it that way.

the last laugh

fighting cancer with wit and humor

ROBBY LEE FELDMAN

mother's day, may 9, 2004

All four of Mom's children met in Tampa to celebrate Mother's Day with her in her 83rd year, most of which she spent as a mother. For about two weeks prior to this weekend, we had been noticing that she was struggling with comprehension of simple things. For instance, she told Geri that, on a phone call to the airlines, the person from U.S. Air just kept talking and wouldn't let her get in a word. Geri figured out that it was a recording that Mom thought was a live person.

So, in the couple weeks before Mother's Day, the four of us called her every day to make sure she was okay. We also agreed to watch her carefully over Mother's Day weekend to see if something needed to be done.

Geri and her husband, Pat, were the first to arrive at Mom's condo and they hadn't seen her in a few months. When they let themselves in and found her on the sofa, they were shocked. She just looked up at them with a blank stare and barely acknowledged them, as if they had simply left the room for a few minutes and were returning.

At the end of the weekend, the four of us knew quite well that something was wrong with her, but didn't know how serious it was, what was causing it, or what we should do about it. So Geri agreed to stay in Tampa another week and make an assessment, along with D. Jay, who lives there.

Towards the end of the week, Mom went out for her daily morning walk in the neighborhood. A half-hour later, Geri got a phone call from a woman saying that Mom had tried to get into her backyard and that she was "confused."

Geri and D. Jay took her to the hospital, which was a short trip...but the beginning of a very long and very difficult journey.

The Hospital

Mom was now in the hospital to find out what was wrong with her. As you might expect from someone with a fiercely independent nature, she didn't adjust too well to the hospital. Nor did it adjust too well to her. In retrospect, we realized that being in a strange environment exaggerated her quickly growing list of cognitive impairments.

Who likes hospitals anyway? Just the food itself is a good reason not to stay around. Plus, she was hooked up to some type of intrusive electronic device which the nursing staff said was a heart monitor. We suspected it was actually something to make you believe the food tasted good. Sort of an electronic taste bud lobotomy device.

One thing that began happening in the hospital is Mom started having frequent obsessions. Yeah, it's true that she always had her share of neuroses, but this was different. She'd get obsessed with an idea (no matter how illogical) and get stuck on it for an hour or more.

May 20, 2004

Mom decided the bed sheet was a big white shirt and kept trying to find the arm holes. This went on for about an hour. She sees a large male nurse and says he could wear the shirt, it would fit him. Then two hours later, she has been medicated and is falling asleep when the same large male nurse comes in to check on her, then leaves after a few moments.

MOM: He forgot to take his shirt.

Mom has been taking a blood thinner for a couple months. One side effect is bruising and Mom has several very large bruises on both arms.

OTHER PATIENT: What's that on your arm?
MOM: A tattoo.
PATIENT: A tattoo of what?
MOM: A tattoo of a bruise.

MOM: I haven't used my Medicare for 19 years, now I'm overusing it.
ROB: You're finally getting your money's worth.
MOM: (She says an expression in Yiddish, I ask what it means, she explains): Good luck struck me.

The Last Laugh

May 21, 2004

The hospital stay was difficult for everyone, mostly for Mom, of course. Her ability to walk was impaired and she was not only obsessing, but also hallucinating (and not about playing golf). Geri, D. Jay, and I stayed by her side. Many times, I'd hold her arm to steady her and we'd walk very, very slowly around the hospital floor, usually with tears streaming down my face. The staff probably was wondering what my Mom had done to make me cry. If they had seen her even a month before, they would've understood immediately.

The Last Laugh

Mom always loved dancing, especially ballroom dancing. For a couple decades after her husband died, she'd go to The Coliseum dance hall in St. Petersburg for the Saturday night dance. As always, men were attracted to Mom. In fact, she was a man magnet. No doubt she loved the attention. But she really went for the dancing.

In the hospital lounge after slowly shuffling down the hall:
ROB (kidding): Mom, do you want to dance?
MOM: Do you want to play professional football?

Waiting for a CAT scan, Mom and I are walking the hospital hallway. She continuously drifts to the left side of the hall. I tell her many times to walk in the center of the hall.

ROB: Either you're listing to the left or the building is leaning to the left.
MOM: I hope the building isn't leaning, my CAT scan will be cock-eyed.

They bring in a new roommate to share Mom's room. The woman coughs loudly.

MOM: Uh-Oh, we're in for trouble.

The Last Laugh

Mom's new roommate is a Hispanic woman. Mom picks up the newspaper and starts reading out loud. It isn't on purpose, but the article is about segregating Hispanic school students from the Caucasians. I cringe and hope the roommate doesn't hear. Just then, the roommate again coughs loudly. Of course, hospitals shouldn't segregate Hispanic patients, but maybe those who cough.

The Nursing Facility

About three years ago, Mom had completely readjusted her health insurance policy. It had originally been for assisted living centers and nursing homes, but she changed it to cover home healthcare. Because Mom really loved her condo and wanted to be comforted by the surroundings if she became ill. In more ways than one, this would soon hit home.

But anyone who has dealt with health insurance companies knows that they're always there for you, except when you really need them. By now, we realized the hospital was hurting Mom, not helping. However, the home healthcare company made it difficult for us to get Mom home quickly. So we decided to put her into a nursing facility until we could get the insurance paperwork finalized.

Although Mom was still able to hold normal conversations intermittently, her cognitive abilities eroded further while in the nursing facility and her ability to walk continued to falter. But, through it all, she never complained. Plus, her humor stayed with her, a constant companion and now a weapon against her still undetermined illness which had wounded her so deeply and had stolen her best friend, independence.

May 22, 2004

Mom walks a few steps from her bed to the bathroom. Except that she instead goes to the closet door. The bathroom door is behind her. For ten minutes, she tries to walk into the closet, feels all the walls, insists it's the door to the bathroom. Finally, I show her the bathroom door which was behind her. She realizes she was mistaken, which must have been disturbing, but she covers it with humor.

MOM: I'll be darned if I know how the bathroom door got behind me. When did they move it?

may 23, 2004

Mom's roommate has a broken hip and is in the advanced stages of Alzheimer's. She asks me for some water, which I give her, then I go back to Mom's bedside.

ROOMATE: This is so good.
MOM (who hadn't seen what I had given the roommate): What's so good?
ROB: The water she's drinking.
MOM: Okay, as long as it isn't a highball.

We are talking about Mom not wanting to take sleep medication. She has always been paranoid of getting addicted to prescription medications.

ROB: Does it bother you to take the medication?
MOM: Yes, but it's not worth losing sleep over.

I introduce Mom to a nice man named David who is in a motorized cart/wheelchair. Mom and I are walking down the hall towards her room. David stops, offers Mom a ride on his motorized wheelchair.

DAVID: Want a ride on my lap?
MOM: No thanks, I don't like convertibles.

The Last Laugh

Since I turned 49, I've had trouble admitting my age. Mom and I are in the dining room, a cute young nurse asks my age, I kind of delay and stutter, finally saying, 49. Mom realizes I didn't want to admit my age.

MOM: Well, you finally spit that out.

may 23, 2004

D. Jay and I were asked to take Mom to a neurosurgeon. He was dressed very casually, wearing Dockers. Which wasn't really a problem, but the "Little Mermaid" lapel pin he was wearing didn't exactly inspire complete confidence. Nor did it when Mom lay down on his examination table because he used her pants as a pillow. It was also disturbing that the one chair in the room had a damaged arm. But this was a "head" doctor, not an "arm" doctor, so D. Jay and I overlooked it.

DR. *(shining a light in her eye):* Look at my nose.
MOM: You have a cute little nose.

DR. *(part of exam, scratches her foot):* Sorry if that's uncomfortable.
MOM: That's okay, I had an itch anyway.

may 24, 2004

In the nursing facility's dining room, Mom is trying to read her diet card without her glasses. The card designates her diet as "regular."

MOM: I'm regal.

Mom doesn't like taking any kind of medication. The nurse, Tina, is patiently trying to get her to take her meds.

ROB: Come on Mom, take your pills. Tina has to go.
MOM (still not taking them): She can go.

ROB: I'm going home to make some calls. Either Barry or me will be back after lunch.
MOM *(correcting my grammar):* Barry or I.
ROB: Speak for yourself.
MOM: Then who'll speak for you?

One thing that carried over from the hospital to the nursing home is Mom's distaste for the food, she said it all tasted the same to her. Funny, really, because Mom never cared much about food. When we kids were growing up, she always cooked big, four-course meals. But after her husband died and her kids left home, Mom spent her independent adulthood seemingly practicing a philosophy that "You should never spend longer preparing a meal than it takes to eat it." Luckily, Mom was a painfully slow eater, so that opened up her options.

At most meals, Mom says, "Everything tastes the same." I bring in Chinese food to share; I'd get half her meal, she'd get half the Chinese food. She doesn't eat any Chinese food. At first, she puts butter on her cod fillet (thinking it was tarter sauce). Then, a few bites later, she puts soy sauce on it. Finally, a few bites later, duck sauce.

MOM: Finally, a meal that tastes different from the rest.

At dinner, Mom gets a fortune cookie, she opens it, reads it to herself.

ROB: What does it say?
MOM (as if she's speaking Chinese): Yung su, yak, yak, yak.

The Last Laugh

At dinner, after mentioning the overcooked food for a week.

MOM: They've cooked the hell out of this stuff.

Mom doesn't particularly like the nurses attending to her and watching her every move.

MOM: Yesterday, I went out to the patio to see the squirrels.
ROB: Did you go alone?
MOM: No, one of the bodyguards went with me.

june 1, 2004

Mom is walking the halls, a bit unsteady and carrying her pillow.

ROB: Mom, why are you carrying the pillow?
MOM: In case I run into something.

There are plenty of fine words out there, that when paired with another word, hit you like an atomic bomb without the subtlety. For instance, "Irreconcilable Differences," "Pink Slip," and "Sick Child."

"Brain Cancer" is another one.

This was when we finally found out what Mom's illness was, but wished we hadn't. To us kids, it was a slap in the face. A shot across the bow. A party crasher of colossal proportion.

But to Mom, it was something else. It was a call to arms.

You see, Mom had entered the arena twice with cancer and had defeated it both times. That's why she couldn't think of any reason this would be different. Of course, she wasn't thinking too clearly at the time.

Regardless, Mom knew she was in a fight. And she was armed and ready. One of those weapons was her sense of humor, honed and polished over decades like a Japanese Samurai sword, and now ready for a fight. Not only the fight of her life, but the fight for her life.

june 3, 2004

Earlier that day, D. Jay had make a joke about telling Mom the story of Besheba. Many hours later, that evening, Mom was going to sleep.

GER: You want me to tell you a bedtime story?
MOM: Yes.
GER: Which one?
MOM: The story of Besheba.

june 4, 2004

Geri is with Mom in the doctor's assistant's office which is extremely, almost comically cluttered, but the assistant is very efficient and helpful.

ASSISTANT: Excuse my office, it's a mess. (she leaves the room)
GER: It seems she really enjoys her work.
MOM: She must, to work in this office.

Unfortunately, Mom has a serious fall in the nursing home. She goes back into the hospital, which again is a hideous experience for her, and I'm not talking about the food. She continually tries to rip the IV out of her arm, constantly hallucinates, can't sleep, and often can't feed herself. In the next two days, we are finally able to finalize the home healthcare insurance, so Mom goes home. Which is really good news. Or bad. Depending on how you look at it.

At Home

 The fall Mom had in the nursing facility has taken a serious toll. Always afraid of heights, now she is afraid of something much more mundane. Walking.

 It's hard to imagine how frightening it must be to fall, especially at age 83. But, over the next weeks, we don't have to use our imagination. It's obvious. In her body language, in her pained facial expressions, and in her dwindling spirit. Although, still, she doesn't complain.

 This also marks a time when everything else continues to decline. Mom is slightly more stable and is hallucinating less at home, but her ability to interact meaningfully continues to falter. It becomes increasingly difficult for Mom to formulate thoughts and put together sentences.

 She seems to understand everything, but cannot interact most of the time. The inability to interact may, in fact, be more difficult to deal with than the inability to walk. Now, she needs help to do both.

june 10, 2004

Geri uses a spoon to give Mom her vitamins.

ROB: Where did you learn that?
GER: Lara (brother D. Jay's wife) did it last night.
ROB (joking): She does that for D. Jay, too…Honey, here's your Viagra.
MOM (looking at the vitamins she's about to take): This is Viagra?

At this point, Mom can't even walk alone. It's dinner time, Geri and I are trying to get her off the couch, she's lying down.

    GER: Okay, put one leg over (the side of the couch).
Mom crosses her legs, moves one leg over a few inches, then crosses her legs opposite from before. No attempt to get off the couch.
    GER: How do you want to get off the couch?
    MOM: In one piece.

She is sitting on the edge of her bed, but doesn't seem to want to lie down.

MOM: Okay, I gotta get going.
ROB: Where you going...dancing, jogging, soccer practice?
MOM (in Yiddish): When the Red Sea parts again.

june 11, 2004

Sitting on the side of her bed after taking off her socks, a few minutes pass, she blows her nose into one of the socks.

MOM: This Kleenex smells.

Geri had been with Mom for eight days, four alone. Geri, Mom and I were at the dining room table.

ROB: Ger, you get the prize for taking care of Mom alone for four days.
GER: It was my pleasure.
MOM: It was your pleasure, so you can keep doing it.

She wants to transfer from her wheelchair, to sit on the couch, but keeps delaying, so I lie down on the couch.

MOM: Be careful or I'll sit on your head.

june 12, 2004

Waking up in the morning, she asks for water.

ROB: Water is one of the three things that you need to live, do you know what the other two are? (food & air)
MOM: Elimination.
ROB: Close, but what was it before it was ready for elimination (a hint that it was food)?
MOM: Shit.

The Last Laugh

The night before, Geri and I had gone out and left Mom with the caregiver. When we got back, I had to lift her into bed and she accidentally peed on me. This is the next morning.

ROB: Were you upset last night that Ger and I went out to dinner?
MOM: No, that was okay.
(few minutes later) ROB: Did you realize you peed on me?
MOM: Well, maybe I was a bit upset you left, but not that upset.

Finished using the toilet, she is having a hard time standing up.

ROB: Mom, you want help, or do you want to stand up by yourself.
MOM: God forbid.

The doctors have said that they don't know if Mom has lymphoma, which is treatable, or glyoma, which is not. The only way to find out is to undergo six weeks of radiation and see if it responds. The odds of it being treatable lymphoma vs. untreatable glyoma, are ten to one. Odds that are formidable even for Mom, who is an undying optimist. At least we hope she is.

june 13, 2004

Sitting on the toilet, not enough strength to get up by herself.

NURSE: Just stand up.
MOM: Sure, loan me your legs.

june 14, 2004

We're waiting in a doctor's little office, she's in wheelchair, facing a completely blank wall.

MOM: I'll just sit back and enjoy the view.

Talking about being sweet vs. being mean.

ROB: You always told us that you get more flies with honey vs. vinegar.
MOM: That works…if you want flies.

june 15, 2004

On port-a-let, defecating profusely.

GER: There's a lot coming out.
MOM: In this case, better out than in.

june 16, 2004

ROB: Mom, we love you.
MOM: It's a good thing you do.
ROB: Why?
MOM: Cause I'd be a nuisance if you didn't.

Nurse cleaning up Mom after using the toilet.

ROB: Mom, your recovery starts with getting enough food and water.
(pause)
ROB: So where does it all start?
MOM: Apparently with my butt.

My last trip down to Tampa, Mom and I had talked about our shared lack of hand strength and I told her about squeezing a tennis ball to build it up. This trip, I bring from Nashville a purple stress ball. I give it to her six or eight times, every single time she puts it down immediately.

ROB: You don't like it?
MOM: No, I don't…but I'll cherish it until the day I die.
ROB: Where do you want me to put it so you can cherish it?
MOM: In that drawer.

june 17, 2004

When I lift her from her port-a-let to the wheelchair, she usually has to put her arms around my neck to hold on, but doesn't like this dependence at all. We're trying to move her and she is annoyed that she needs help.

ROB: You want to put your arms around my neck?
MOM: How about around your throat?

She won't eat anything substantial, so we give her one of her favorites, toast with cheese on it.

MOM: It tastes like cardboard with cheese on it. (pause) But I'm not complaining, it's particularly good cardboard.

Geri is getting the port-a-let ready for her, not knowing that she's already soiled her diaper.

GER: I've got this for you.
MOM: I've got something for *you*.

The Last Laugh

Mom has done nothing but eat, drink, and sleep for days, when D. Jay comes to visit.

D. JAY: Hi, what did you do today?
MOM (faux slang): I didn't do nuthin'.

We've been reading the book, *Joys of Yiddish* together. She has loved reading for many years, but hasn't been able to read for a month, due to the brain tumor. Not being able to read is extremely disturbing to her.

ROB: I'm gonna go read the paper.
MOM: You can read?
ROB: Yeah.
MOM: Paskudneh! *(A Yiddish word meaning contemptible)*

june 18, 2004

Mom is in bed, I am lightly tapping her arm, affectionately.

MOM *(annoyed by this):* What's the tapping for?
ROB: It's Morse Code for, "I love you."
MOM: What happened, you can't talk anymore?

There's a decorative plaque on the wall, just as you walk into her condo. It is written in Hebrew.

ROB: What does that mean?
MOM: Welcome.
ROB: So it welcomes guests?
MOM: Only Hebrew guests.

june 19, 2004

ROB: I'm gonna go out and get a newspaper to see if you can read it.
MOM *(sarcastically):* That would be a red letter day.

D. JAY: Mom, are you tired?
MOM: Tired of doing nothing.

july 1, 2004

In transit to a radiation treatment, she's babbling incoherently.

> *MOM:* So what about the board?
> *D. JAY:* The board, I don't know what you mean.
> *MOM:* Neither do I.

ROB: My friend is a Nestle rep who sells a medical nutritional drink, especially for radiation patients. She has sent us a free case of it. It's really tasty and good for your health.
MOM: And it's a good price, too.

JACKIE (caregiver): I'll put the casserole in the freezer.
MOM: Good, so we can resurrect it later.

Son Barry boards, sells, and trains horses for a living.
Mom is talking with him on the phone, I'm on the extension.

ROB: Mom, ask Barry how his horses are.
MOM: Who cares?

For weeks, we have been making requests to which she says, "okay," then does nothing. She says it again.

ROB: You know, "okay" has become your favorite word… followed by doing nothing.
MOM: Okay.

july 2, 2004

Following is an email Mom and I composed and sent out to the extended family:

Sent: Friday, July 02, 2004 5:31 PM
Subject: Letter from Eleanor

Dear Friends, Family, and Various Hackers,

As you know, I'm a little bit under the weather. But, living in Florida during the summer, that's to be expected, right?

Geri has mentioned several times that you'all (a Southern expression that includes everyone but hackers) have been asking about me.

Other than the weather, things are not so hot. But I want you to know I'm not in any pain, although my life is kind of a pain in the ass if you want the truth.

For instance, people keep making me eat even when I'm not hungry. They force me to get out of bed even when I don't want to. They shower me with attention even when I don't need a shower.

(Continued)

Seriously, though, it's a rough time, especially not knowing what's around the next corner. I just keep walking straight ahead and try not to think about the corners too much. Actually, I guess that's pretty much what I've done all along.

We've had ("we" being what nurses refer to as "medicinal third person" grammar) eight radiation treatments with maybe ten or so more to go. They seem to be helping, but, frankly, it's hard to tell. On a day-to-day basis, everything is such a roller coaster anyway. Now I know why roller coasters made me sick.

There's really not much else to report for now. Except that I do very much appreciate all your calls and all your thoughts, even though I can't respond in the way I'd like to. Just knowing that you care is enough for me. I hope it's enough for you.

That's it for this report, someone is trying to make me eat again.

Thanks,
Love,
El

Trying to get her out of bed, into the wheelchair.

ROB: Come on, Mom, we're going on a trip.
MOM: Trips are good (then whispers) unless they're bad.

I sneeze.

MOM: Is there a dog barking?

She can't read, but doesn't want to admit it. I show her something to see if she can read it.

ROB: Mom, what does this say (she doesn't answer, I repeat this four times).
MOM: I don't know, but it's annoying.

july 3, 2004

Today is Mom's birthday. Her 84th. The celebration is a bit muted because we realize there may not be an 85th.

Mom's friend Irene is visiting. She often gives advice to her grown children, which she and Mom have discussed many times.

> *IRENE:* My daughter bought a bed & breakfast but she didn't tell me about it until afterwards.
> *MOM:* That was wise of her.

Irene reading a birthday greeting that says, "Happy birthday, you're always the star of our show." Irene tries to get Mom to read it, prompting her.

IRENE: You're always…
MOM: Right.

⁓

IRENE: Happy birthday to you.
MOM: Happy birthday to me.

D. Jay takes a lot of time and effort to make birthday dinner for her while she sits and watches. After dinner.

ROB: Pretty good dinner, huh, Mom?
MOM: Yeah, and with very little effort. (meaning her effort)

july 4, 2004

Slept most of the day, except to get her diapers changed. At dinner.

ROB: Mom, you've had a heck of a day.
MOM (gestures): Quality. Quality. Quality.

july 5, 2004

TECHNICIAN *after taking Mom's blood pressure:*
You have good blood pressure.
MOM: Thank You

ROB: Do you want to get out of bed and into the wheelchair and come supervise while I make lunch?
MOM: Yes
ROB: Are you ready?
MOM: Yes.
After several minutes of her not moving an inch.
ROB: You're saying you're ready but you're not moving.
MOM: Sure I am, but I move slowly.

Waiting in the waiting room to be called in for her radiation treatment, Mom is getting fidgety and trying to get out of the wheelchair. I try to distract her by getting her to do arm exercises, putting both arms out to the side and rotating them in circles. I'm doing them, but she isn't following along.

ROB: Won't you do these exercises with me?
MOM: No
ROB: But I look foolish doing them alone.
MOM: Better one of us looking foolish than two. Someone has to protect the family name.

july 6, 2004

For several minutes Mom is trying to get out of her wheelchair when she shouldn't be. D. Jay is kneeling in front of her, holding her legs so she can't get up. Finally she stands up. Then, so does D. Jay, they are now standing very close together, facing each other. Mom is hemmed in, can't go anywhere.

MOM: O.K., I'm going to do something now.
D. JAY: What are you going to do?
MOM: I'm going to shake your hand.
She reaches out does so, then immediately sits back down in her chair.

Mom says she's tired, so we put her into bed. She closes her eyes and almost immediately opens them.

MOM: That was the fastest nap I ever had.

After trying many times to do something and finally getting it right.

MOM: I have it firmly in-crunched in my brain.

Mom, not in Rob's presence, calls him a "fat ass."
(He is actually very thin)

GER: Can I tell him you called him a fat ass?
MOM: Yes, we never keep secrets from the kids.

The word "dreck" in Yiddish means something that is bad, unusable, disgusting. Mom is taking a medication that may be muddling her brain even more than the tumor. It's called Decadron. Out of the blue, she calls it "Dreck-a-dron."

july 7, 2004

Geri brings Mom a pair of hot pink knit pants.

> *GER:* Do they feel good, Mom?
> *MOM:* Yes
> *GER:* They're a good color for you.
> *MOM:* Yes, I always liked blue.

The Last Laugh

Much earlier in the day, D. Jay was trying to entertain Mom by singing the song, "do the Hokey Pokey." Later, Mom begins to fall asleep on the couch and D. Jay tells Mom he'll lift her into her wheelchair to take her to her bed. He tells Mom to put her arms around his neck so he can lift her. She is really sleepy and not doing so.

GER *(to a woman who went ballroom dancing weekly for many years of her life)*: Mom, put your arms around D. Jay's neck and pretend you're dancing. What dance would you like to do?
MOM: The Hokey Pokey.

Mom was laying in bed shredding a diaper, one of her obsessive behaviors. I asked her why she was doing that; she looked at me with a totally blank expression for about 10 seconds and then said "Do I have to have a reason?"

Overheard Mom say during a phone conversation:
"I acted very busy today."

Mom's sitting at the dining room table in her wheelchair. I have it pulled very close to the table and the brakes are locked so that she can't get up from the chair, although she keeps trying.

MOM: How can I get extricated?

Mom, D. Jay and I are coming out of Moffit Cancer Center after a radiation treatment, D. Jay pushing Mom in her wheelchair. We pass several people coming in as we were going out.

MOM: They do a rousing business here!

july 9, 2004

Mom, mostly uninterested in food, is losing weight at an alarming rate and is now under 100 pounds. She is skeletal with sunken eyes and protruding bones. Very disturbing for a woman who was always impeccable about her looks. At this point, her ability to understand is still very good, but her ability to interact seems to get steadily worse. As for food and conversation, I'm sure she's starved for at least one of those.

july 15, 2004

Caregiver putting Mom on the port-a-let.
Ger pointedly leaves the room.

GER: See you later.
MOM: You're sure a fair weathered friend.

Walking with her good friend, Irene, Mom is wearing a bad wig.

GER: What do you think you look like with that wig?
MOM: I look like shit.

Ger gives Mom socks to put on, she fiddles, Ger prompts her.

GER: Are you gonna put your socks on your feetsies?
MOM *(with mock sarcasm):* No, on my earsies.

july 16, 2004

ROB: Do you want the pillow you're using, or the one that's more firm?
MOM: Decisions, decisions, decisions.

Facakta is a Yiddish word meaning discombobulated. She is unknowingly putting on a sock over another sock. She struggles for a few minutes, then finally quits.

MOM: This is one facakta sockta.

july 17, 2004

She won't eat lunch. I get up to get a drink for myself.

ROB: I suggest you spend this time contemplating how you're gonna eat that burger.
When I come back, she's hidden the burger under a napkin.

She hiccups.

ROB: Excuse you.
MOM: And you.

Scratching her arm.

ROB: What're you doing?
MOM: I have an itch.
ROB *(kidding, quoting Martin Luther King)*: I have a dream.
MOM: To each his own.

Trying to get Mom to gain weight, we're putting high protein powder in every concoction. We give her oatmeal with Boost and cut up power bars in it.

ROB: Do you like it?
MOM: It's pretty good for crap.

july 19, 2004

Mom and I composed another email to the extended family:

Sent: Monday, July 19, 2004 1:44 AM
Subject: Macaroons

Dear Friends, Family, and Supporters of the Patriot Act (because we know They're always watching),

It's raining here in Tampa, a nice respite from the heat. Unfortunately, it's coincidentally quite wet. Making it difficult for me to get to soccer practice or the golf driving range.

Speaking of rain, it's been raining good news recently (to mangle a metaphor, which I reserve the right to do in my current condition).

The follow-up MRI Wednesday - after about 14 radiation treatments – showed that the tumor (I hate that word so from now on we'll call it a macaroon) has shrunken significantly. Meaning that the macaroon is a lymphoma…which is treatable. The odds against this were about 9 to 1. In fact, if any of you need stock advice, feel free to call.

The Last Laugh

My Oncologist, the resplendent Dr. Aurebach, has recommended a new form of chemo that has very few side effects. Again, pretty darn lucky considering I probably couldn't have tolerated traditional chemo. Sort of like I can't tolerate American cheese on white toast.

More good stuff. I'm walking with the help of a walker (I hate that word so let's call it the facakta ambulation machine). Am using a real toilet with raised seat which feels like a throne. Am going for wheelchair walks in the neighborhood, deftly getting past the condo guard gate in what we like to call a jail break. And am still bossing around everyone who shows any remote interest in following my various requests.

Speaking of requests, my request for everyone would be to avoid macaroons at all costs.

Love to all,
El

august 12, 2004

Mom is obsessed with putting a towel around her head, like a scarf. Everything but her face is covered up.

ROB: You would make a beautiful Afghani woman.
MOM: Finally I found a niche for myself.

august 13, 2004

Mom has been snoozing on the couch for a while. Finally she says, "I should get off my duff and do something."

ROB: If you got off your duff to do something, what would you do?
MOM: I'd look for a new place for my duff.

D. Jay is walking up the condo hallway with Mom who is using her walker. She has walked further than she normally does.

D. JAY: You're a walking fool today.
MOM: I was a fool yesterday, too.

Everything has changed.

After a couple weeks on the cancer chemo drug, it turns out that Mom can no longer take it. We are shell shocked. It's hard to tell, but she certainly is, too. This is unfamiliar territory for Mom, not winning the fight.

It is wrenching to see her at this point. Extremely skinny. Frail. A dull, far-away look in her eyes (when they're open, which isn't often). After losing the ability to walk, eat by herself, consistently communicate, etc, now she is losing something even more precious. Her will to live.

Regrettably, all we can do is keep Mom comfortable and make sure she realizes that she is loved. Amazingly, she is still stoic, never complaining. When asked if she's okay, she says "Yes." When asked if she's comfortable, she says "Yes." When asked if there's anything we can do, she says, "Just be here."

In essence, all we can do is help Mom die. Ironic considering she spent most of her life helping us live.

august 28, 2004

Grace, Mom and I at dining room table, after lunch. Grace is telling me all sorts of things about Mom's care, goes on for 5 or 6 minutes.

GRACE *(to Mom):* Are we talking about you too much?
MOM: No, just enough.

august 29, 2004

Sitting at table. Barry had called earlier.

ROB: Barry called earlier to ask about you for a few minutes.
MOM: Why did I get only a few minutes?

august 30, 2004

I take Mom out in her wheelchair to the neighborhood that she walked in every single day for 12 years. The sidewalks are bumpy.

MOM: Why is it so bumpy?
ROB: Well, the sidewalks are bumpy. But isn't it beautiful...the trees...the brick streets...the birds?
MOM: Yes, it is. Guess sometimes you just have to overlook the bumps in the road to enjoy the nice things.
ROB: Yes. Yes, indeed.

In the den, I'm watching TV and she is pretending to. I ask her which channel she wants, she says 22. Fifteen minutes later, I say let's play a game; she chooses a channel number and I will turn to it.

ROB: What number do you want me to turn to?
MOM: 22.
ROB: Mom, that's the channel we're on. What, you think you raised a stupid son?
MOM: Yes.
ROB: Which one?
MOM (giggles): I'm not saying.

Mom sometimes blurts out words that seem like nonsense.

MOM: Fisticuffs.
ROB: Are you threatening me?
MOM: Better believe it.

We're now watching a TV show about the space shuttle, they say the Earth is 2/3 water.

ROB: Did you know the Earth is 2/3 water?
MOM: Of course.
ROB: What's the other 1/3?
MOM: Land.
ROB: No, it's gin.
MOM: Then the rest should be tonic, not water.

august 31, 2004

Uncommon now, she has a little bit of energy, so I give her some choices how to use it...take a shower, walk, talk to me. She doesn't answer.

ROB: You want me to decide for you?
MOM: That'd be passing the buck.
ROB: I wouldn't mind that, I could use a buck.
MOM: But I would, you know how frugal I am.

Trying to help put Mom's shoe on, awkwardly.

ROB: I haven't done this before. I try to avoid people's feet whenever possible.
MOM: See, you're not the stupid son.

Mom can't walk without a walker and then only a few steps a day. She can't control her elimination. She can't read. Or watch TV. Worst of all, she can't communicate. This despite the fact she seems to understand everything. It is really the worst of both worlds.

When Mom first went home, we had a hospital bed delivered to make it easier for her. I am sitting in a chair, beside the bed, looking through the metal side rails at Mom. She looks very frail, very weak, very tired.

Looking at her through the bed rails, they remind me of prison bars and I realize the one thing that we never thought would happen to our Mom and the last thing you'd want to realize about anyone you love:

That Mom had now become a prisoner in a life that she no longer wanted to live.

september 25, 2004

Sitting at the dining room table, tears in my eyes. Mom is holding my hand, to comfort me as much, or more, as for herself.

ROB: I'm so happy to be here, but it's difficult. Understand?
MOM: Yes.
After 10 or 15 minutes, she's still holding my hand.
ROB: Mom, will you let go of my hand so I can go to the bathroom?
MOM: No.

september 26, 2004

Mom is in her wheelchair, the dining room table in front of her, a wall behind her. She tries to push her chair away from the table.

>ROB: Do you want to get away from the table?
>MOM: Yes.
>ROB: Where do you want to go?
>MOM: To the right or to the left.

In bed, falling asleep for a nap.

ROB: Mom, you wanna rest alone for 10 or 15 minutes?
MOM: No, why waste 10 or 15 minutes?

epilogue

As of this writing, my Mom is still alive. But, unfortunately, hardly living. At least the life that would make her happy and fulfilled. The worst part, perhaps, is that she can no longer communicate much. Which means no more of her sharp wit, soothing humor, and girlish giggle. As difficult as it is for us not to have those things to console us during these troubled times, I can assure you it is much more difficult for her.

However, Mom has always been an inspiration. And still is. As you've seen from these vignettes, she has fought the cancerous invasion of her brain with every fiber of her being. Using her sharp wit as both a weapon and a security blanket. Not only for her, but for us, too.

In addition, she has never complained once during her illness, no matter how wrenching it was for her.

As Mom nears her final days, we hope that her example will encourage other people to die with dignity and humor as she did. But, much more important, we hope that her example will encourage you to live that way, too.

post-epilogue

Although we thought Mom would be with us for another couple months, she died two days after (almost exactly to the hour) I wrote the Epilogue. Geri was there, by her side and comforting her during the final minutes. Mom died quickly, peaceably, and with no pain. She didn't say anything. But she did smile. And I'd guess that, if she could have, she would've laughed.

It would have been the last laugh.

Eleven days later, there was a full eclipse of the moon and I was watching, enthralled. The moon was so bright, you could hardly look at it. Then the earth's shadow began blocking out the glowing moon slowly. Very slowly.

It made me think of Mom's final few months. Her special luminescence being slowly obstructed and finally hidden from view.

For a few minutes, this made me very sad and the sky turned into an impressionistic painting, blurred by the tears in my eyes.

Then the moon broke through the shadow, glowing brighter than ever.

I realized that we'd never have our Mom's humor anymore.

But we'd always have her spirit.

personal stories of eleanor's children

barry

When I was about 14 years old, I got into the dating thing. Well, sort of. Don't remember actually going out on an actual date, but we called it dating. Anyway I ended up asking a girl to go steady and we exchanged rings. I was apprehensive about how Mom and Dad would react and tried very hard to figure out the best way to tell them. One day I was in the kitchen talking to Mom about something. I had my hand with the ring on it hidden in some fashion as I had not yet broken the news. Without letting me know that she had spotted the ring, Mom said to me, "Congratulations on going steady. Who is the lucky girl?"

At some point in my senior year at the University of Florida, I realized that I was on my way to becoming an accountant, something that I had no desire to do. I was majoring in accounting as an avenue to law school and decided not to pursue that career. I made the decision to change to a major in Recreation and to drop out of school the first trimester. I really thought that Mom would have a fit. An extra year of college, more money spent, a wayward child, etc. I drove home to Tampa to tell her in person and to be a man and face her wrath/disappointment face to face. I told her what I had done and she said quite calmly, "I never did understand why you didn't make a change a long time ago." Of course then I was mad at her for not telling me what to do a long time ago! Like I would have listened!!!

geri

Dad died a few weeks before I graduated from high school. I had been accepted at a college 120 miles from Tampa. Although Mom was a tower of strength from the moment we got the call that Dad had collapsed in his shop, I realized how difficult Mom's life would be without Dad. She had made the decision to go into his antique business rather than sell out to Dad's partner, so she would be working full time. Both Rob, aged 11 and D. Jay, aged 15, remained at home and Mom now had total responsibility for their upbringing. I knew that if I went to a university in Tampa and lived at home, I could relieve Mom of some of the responsibility of taking care of the house, help to some degree with my brothers and be less of a burden financially. I also believed that my being at home would provide Mom with some emotional support. When I told Mom of my decision to apply to a college in Tampa, she wouldn't even entertain the idea. She said that she and Dad together had planned on my going to the University of Florida and that's where I would go. Even at age 17, I realized what a sacrifice Mom was making by insisting that I go away to school—there is no question that her life would have been easier had I stayed at home. And, as I have aged and matured, the magnitude of that sacrifice has become even more clear. She showed such incredible strength in insisting I do what was best for me, rather than what would have been easiest for her.

One of my brothers once said to me that he envied my closeness to our extended family. He's right, I am incredibly fortunate to have close relationships with extended family members. I have Mom to thank for this blessing. Through her actions—traveling many miles to be at all the special occasions of her extended family—she modeled for me how to cultivate such family ties. Mom always had a large circle of friends which were a very important part of her life. But, nothing was as important as her family!

"One Bam" was my favorite call. All through my childhood, Mom played Mah-jongg once a week with the same five women and I would hear the clack of tiles and strange calls from my bedroom. In addition, this group frequently socialized as couples and remained close friends for scores of years. One of the ways I learned the value of friendships and how to nurture ongoing relationships was by watching Mom build and maintain her friendships.

By the time I was diagnosed with cancer in the spring of 2002, traveling had become difficult for Mom and she was content to stay at home and have her children come to visit her. However, she insisted on coming to visit me in Virginia after my first chemotherapy treatment to help take care of me. The trip wasn't easy for her. And, she arrived to see one of her precious children struggling with the awful side effects of chemotherapy. For the first couple of days after my treatment, I could do little more than lie on the couch. When I wasn't sleeping, I didn't even have enough energy to carry on a conversation. Mom sat for hours watching me dozing or lying awake silently on the couch, at the ready to jump up to get me something to eat or drink whenever I felt I could do either. At the time, I knew that the traveling wasn't easy for her and was extremely grateful to her for making the effort to come to be with me. And, though I knew that it had to be very difficult watching one of her children suffering, I didn't realize what an emotional toll that must have taken on her until our roles were reversed and I was in the position of watching Mom suffer from the ravages of her brain cancer.

As hard as that entire experience must have been for Mom, she made the trip again, after my last chemotherapy treatment. Knowing what she might face, that second trip must have been even harder for her. However, as always, Mom put aside her own well-being in order to tend to the needs of one of her children.

***

Try as I might, Mom has one trait I was never ever to emulate. Though certainly not unfeeling, Mom is stoic. She's had some very significant challenges in her life, yet I have seldom seen her shed tears. By watching her, I have learned how to get through difficult situations but, unfortunately, I never learned from her how to do it without tears!

***

Recently one of my brothers relayed a conversation he had had with a friend from high school whom he hadn't seen in a while. After telling his friend that our mother was gravely ill, his friend expressed his sorrow about Mom's condition. In response, my brother said that Mom was 84 years old, had had a good life and, until recently, had been quite healthy. I thought about this for a few minutes then pointed out to my brother that, in addition to other not inconsequential challenges, Mom had breast cancer twice, lost her husband when she was in her 40's and she was left with the responsibility of completing the raising and educating of her four children. Because of the way Mom responded to these life-changing and life-threatening situations, it appears she had an easy life. From my Mom I learned how to meet adversity with strength and how to move forward and not dwell on things you cannot change.

As Mom's illness progressed, it became more and more difficult for her to rouse herself and get out of bed. The last night of one of my visits, I went into Mom's room to find her dozing. I asked if she would get out of bed and come sit with me awhile since I would be leaving in the morning. Although it was obvious that what Mom really wanted was to remain comfortably in her bed, she exerted a tremendous amount of energy, sat up in bed, allowed me to help her into her wheelchair and push her into the dining room where we sat together for a time. She was, for the most part, incapable of expressing her love verbally by this point, but, by the effort she exerted getting out of bed, her feelings were crystal clear.

During the first three months after Mom's diagnosis of brain cancer, I had spent more time with her in Tampa than I had at home. During one of my visits she had to drink 8 ounces of Citrate of Magnesium, a foul tasting medication that made her gag and her eyes water. She could only take a few sips at a time so it took a long time to finish the glass. It was awful for me watching her struggle to get it down. When she had drunk about three fourths of the glass, in an infrequent moment of total lucidity, she took my hand, looked at me and said, "I'm so glad you're here with me." Those few words made everything I had given up to be with her inconsequential.

When I was about 22 years old, I "fell in love" for the first time. It was quite a fall. But when we broke up, it was an even bigger fall. Had never experienced anything quite like that. As always, was comforted by my best friend and closest confident, my Mom. Of course, she had been through some major heartaches herself, including losing her husband at age 47. Again, as usual, she listened patiently (on every phone call for weeks) and offered endless empathy. When she sensed I had made it through the worst of it and really wanted to get my life back on track, she offered a simple yet elegant observation that I never forgot, even to this day. She said, "Sometimes, Rob, the only cure for a woman is another woman."

―――

At age eight, I tried out for a competitive baseball team, one that you have to have a certain level of skills to join. I didn't make it and, of course, was pretty upset. Mom doesn't particularly like whiners, even kids, I guess. But she let me vent a little bit, then sat me down and pulled up a chair. As she looked into my eyes, Mom said there was no need to be upset or embarrassed or ashamed. She said, "It's not so much what you do…it's what you try to do."

―――

My favorite toy at age five was a plastic action figure of Popeye. I loved it. The arms moved in their sockets. One day, I accidentally pulled one of the arms out of its socket and we couldn't fix it. I cried (still do cry when something I love is broken, like my Mom is now). Mom said that we could get another one, but that I should realize that it probably won't be the same. She said that some things can be replaced but we can't replace how we feel about them.

―――

After two years of college, I didn't know what major I wanted to declare. So I told Mom that I wanted to work for five or six months, save money, then move to Denver for a year while I decided what career to pursue. She said quite directly that she didn't like the idea, mostly she was afraid I wouldn't go back and finish college. But she also said she'd support me in any way possible, including driving with me out to Denver if I wanted. I declined that offer although I did take her spirit with me.

Mom, who I think secretly wanted all of us to marry Jewish partners, never put that direct pressure on us, at least not me. When I was living in Japan, she visited me and met my girlfriend who, coincidentally, was Japanese. Mom really loved Mariko, but that's beside the point, I think. When I asked her how she'd feel if I married Mariko, Mom smiled and said that she'd like it anyway…but that the point was for me to be happy, not her.

In the hospital the night before Mom's mastectomy surgery when she was just 52 years old, I noticed she had on a low-cut nightgown. I asked why. She said that, when any male hospital employees came into the room, she "Gave them an eyeful." She said, "As long as I have them, I'm gonna use them."

Mom's only husband, who happened to also be my Dad, died when he was 48, she was 47, and I was 11. About a year later, Mom called me into the family room. With glistening eyes, she carefully told me that she had a date this coming weekend. Of course, it hurt me. And of course, she knew it would. She explained that, no matter what, no one could or would replace Dad for her…or for me. But she said that she had to get on with her life and asked me to understand. Then she asked if I remembered the Popeye toy that had been broken when I was five and I said yes. She said she might someday have another husband but reminded me that, like the toy, the feelings you have for something you love can never be replaced. It took many years before that really sunk in. But right now, as Mom seems to be preparing to depart, her words could never be more crystal clear.

footprints
(five weeks after mom died)

I was on my cement patio tonight wearing sandals. There were small puddles but lots of dry areas, too. When I walked through a puddle and then onto a dry area, the soles of the sandals made a distinctive footprint. But the footprint, because it was just water, quickly disappeared. That was one of the goals of putting together this collection of my Mom's perseverance and humor. Because I don't want her footprints to disappear.

www.ingramcontent.com/pod-product-compliance
Lightning Source LLC
Chambersburg PA
CBHW031357160426
42813CB00090B/3117/J